Perilous Path

a writer's journey

MORE FROM THIS AUTHOR

Mystical Circles
A Passionate Spirit

Perilous Path
a writer's journey

SC SKILLMAN

LUMINARIE

First published in Great Britain in March 2017 by *Blue Lily Press*
This paperback edition published in August 2017 by *Luminarie*

A CIP catalogue record for this book is available from the British Library.

Cover design Annabelle Bradford 2017

ISBN 978-1-9997073-2-3

LUMINARIE

www.scskillman.com
www.luminarie.uk

ACKNOWLEDGEMENTS

Quotations used in this book are from the following sources: article by Alison Baverstock in *The Writers' and Artists' Yearbook*; *Sacred Spaces* by Margaret Silf; a talk by Adrian Plass given during the Scargill Writers Weekend at Scargill House, Yorkshire, in 2016; *Story* by Robert McKee; *Creativity and the Beatles*, an online article by Ayd Instone in his blog aydinstone.wordpress.com; *War and Peace* by Leo Tolstoy; *Pride and Prejudice* by Jane Austen; *Portrait of the Artist as a Young Girl* by Wendy Jones and Grayson Perry; Ernest Hemingway interview in *The Paris Review Interviews*; and words from St Paul in the *NIV Bible*.

DEDICATION

To my loyal blog followers and all those
who have supported and encouraged me on my
writing journey.

CONTENTS

Based on original material by SC Skillman

first published online on

SC Skillman Blog:

Inside the mind of a writer

www.scskillman.com

Review of *Perilous Path*:

'I found it fascinating to read how one new writer began to write, and continued to self-motivate in her determination to achieve her goals – and how her faith provides example and inspiration.

'Some of the articles contain ideas about writing that I haven't considered previously; some of the articles are more like friendly reminders of things I already know, or focus on interests that (like many readers and writers, I imagine) I share with the author.

'Reading the book felt like having a "friend in the room" giving advice and sharing her experiences of the writing process.'

Victoria Lee
Freelance Editor

1 THE WRITER'S JOURNEY: PURSUING YOUR CREATIVE PASSION

After being turned down by numerous publishers,
he had decided to write for posterity.
(George Ade)

It is a truth certainly acknowledged by the author of the above quote that many creative writers struggle for years, enduring perhaps decades in the wilderness of submissions and rejections, before their persistence finally pays off.

"Most would-be authors," says Alison Baverstock in The Writers' and Artists' Yearbook, "are pessimistic optimists."

This is certainly true: so where can we find inspiration from the examples of others, in life, and in the pages of literature?

Take, for instance, some of the characters in the world's greatest stories. The Old Testament is full of accounts of people who waited or fought seemingly in vain or wandered in the wilderness for many years before God's plan for them unfolded, and their gifts were used and they prospered.

Joseph, Moses, and Elijah come to mind. Moses was 80 years old when he led the Children of Israel out of Egypt, and witnessed the parting of the Red Sea. Elijah gave way to depression before God re-commissioned him. Joseph languished forgotten in jail before his gift for interpreting dreams lifted him up again.

Fast forward a few thousand years to my chance meeting with a publisher (later to become one of London's top literary agents) who took an interest in my writing. He encouraged me to write my first novel.

My experience with him reminds me now of an evening I once attended on the subject of 'discernment'. There, an image was presented to us: 'You can spend years knocking on doors. Some doors lead to broom cupboards and some to elevator shafts.'

When I met this publisher, in the early stages of my writing career, I opened a door and it led into a lift. I stepped in, and went up. But it was a faith-operated lift. It required me to have enough faith to press the button for the top floor. I only had enough faith to press the button for the third floor. The doors opened, the demon of self-doubt stepped in, and pressed the button for the basement. And down I went again, to the very bottom of the shaft.

So, as my writing life continued beyond the outer gates, rejections frequently came my way, and I read letters saying things like: "We read this with much amusement but in the end were not sufficiently drawn to the central idea" and "We found your style fluent and assured but it is not quite for us" and "Although this is witty and well written…our fiction programme is so full that we are buying very few new titles unfortunately…I wish you success in finding a less over-burdened publisher."

But I later discovered that, contrary to the feelings of rejected authors, when you actually meet editors in publishing houses, they're very pleasant people. The Mills and Boon editor I met in the Ladies at the Savoy Hotel in London, at the Romantic Novelists Association Romantic Novel of the Year Award luncheon, was very nice. And so was the rights director for the top agent I referred to earlier in this chapter, whom I met later in the dining room. She reminded me of a member of my babysitting circle. (This lady still rejected my novel when I sent it to her though, and subsequently left the agency and published a novel herself).

And so I continued to read letters saying, "Due to the very strong market in this kind of literature your novel would not be viable for us to publish" or "This is too commercial for us," or " I'm afraid this doesn't quite fit with our current list."

Then I read Margaret Silf's book *Sacred Spaces* and found these words in her chapter on 'Crossing Places':

At this 'burial plot' of my experience, I am standing between two worlds – between the old, the known and understood, and the new beginning which still lies beyond the scope of my wildest imagining. I am standing in sacred space because it is on the very edge of the known that the infinite possibilities of the unknown begin to unfold.

She went on to say:

God stretched the rainbow across the heavens, so that we might never forget the promise that holds all creation in being. This is the promise that life and joy are the permanent reality, like the blue of the sky, and that all the roadblocks we encounter are like the clouds — black and threatening perhaps, but never the final word. Because the final word is always "Yes!"

2 RESEARCH FOR FICTION: HOW TO RESEARCH WHEN SOMETHING DOESN'T EXIST

My first thought upon answering this question is, that it does exist – in the writer's imagination. And therefore, it is to the writer's own experience, own memories, own observations and wisdom that we look, to conduct our research. But my second thought is this: when, as a creative writer, you are writing about something that doesn't exist, what is the most desired outcome? It is this: that your readers must – while they are reading your book – believe in it. During the process of engaging with your story, your reader must feel, react, respond, exactly as if this thing does exist. So how do we achieve that?

We make use of a device with a well-established name: 'the willing suspension of disbelief'. It's what happens when we are absorbed in a *Doctor Who* story, or a tale of Arthur and Merlin. It happens to all those who read and love *The Lord of the Rings* or the Narnia stories; and, of course, all successful novels in the fantasy and science fiction genre. As we read, we believe. That's not because we actually think Middle Earth is real, or it is indeed possible to walk through a wardrobe of fur coats into a snow-laden forest. It's because – in view of the powerful story-telling – we willingly suspend our disbelief.

The magic the author uses to achieve this may be found, essentially, in psychological reality. And that may be expressed through truthful characterisation, and classic story structure. Both of these are so important precisely because they correspond to psychological realities in the lives of all of us; and so we recognise them. These are the archetypes that Carl Jung referred to. They may also be identified as 'the tropes' of any particular genre; in other words, the expectations that readers have of this genre, whether or not they are consciously aware of them: the hero, ally, trickster, mentor, wise fool, common man, maze, death-trap, moral trap, hazardous journey, riddle, inmost cave, trophy of conquest.

Such is our faith in classic story structure, that we will believe the story-teller on the basis of it. When we as readers see it is there, we can let our guard down, we can enter into whatever the story-teller has for us, and we can say, "I believe the promises this author makes. I want to know the answers to the questions she poses; and I believe she will provide satisfying answers which will reward me for all the time I spend reading this story."

3 RESEARCH FOR FICTION: USE THE INTERNET

How big a part should the internet play in a novelist's research? My mind is immediately drawn to a quote from Dan Brown's novel *The Lost Symbol.* How often, muses Robert Langdon to himself, has he advised his students that 'Google is not a synonym for research'. I couldn't help laughing at the sly irony of that. For I defy anyone to read this novel without wondering how long the author spent on Google researching his subject matter; and how soon you will get onto Google yourself after reading it, to corroborate his facts – or to fall into the very trap Robert Langdon warns against!

I confess the internet has been a wonderful resource for me as a fiction writer in double-checking my remembered facts. But, of course, we should never assume that what we read on the web is necessarily true. It is important to at least triple-check. But when it comes to writing fiction, I believe most authors will have chosen their subject or theme out of passion – and, therefore, he or she will have spent a considerable portion of their life researching the subject through multifarious means – personal experience, observing and interacting with people, reading all sorts of printed material about it, visiting places, maybe even living out some of the things they depict their characters doing.

Therefore, the internet is a valuable tool, but cannot serve as the sole source of material when researching a novel.

I may take as an example the Cotswolds location for my first published psychological thriller. I was inspired by three places. Firstly, Totleigh Barton at Sheepwash, near Beauworthy in Devon where I once attended a five-day Arvon Foundation poetry course: it boasted a monk's room, as does the farmhouse in my novel. Also, the diverse group of students on the course inspired me for the group dynamics of my story.

Secondly, my imagination was fired by the Lygon Arms Hotel in Broadway in the Cotswolds, a wonderful setting for a psychological thriller. My favourite piece of research involved afternoon tea there. The manager took us for a tour of the most historical rooms in the hotel, including the Cromwell Room. The owners of the inn were neutral during the English Civil War and thus hosted guests on both sides of the conflict. I used some of the details of the interiors here in my descriptions of the sixteenth-century farmhouse.

And thirdly, for my setting, although I ultimately chose the Cotswolds as my favoured location, I was also inspired by a farmhouse near the Forest of Orleans in France owned by the eccentric uncle of my then boyfriend.

We visited his uncle there several years ago. This uncle (now deceased) was a colourful character who had fought on the republican side in the

Spanish Civil War, spent a few years in jail after the war ended, and later fled to Paris after dealing in contraband. When I met him, he displayed a love of practical jokes, leaving plastic rats and spiders for me to find in odd corners. He also owned a parrot, which I came upon by surprise in his sitting room, exactly as I describe my main character coming upon the gold and blue macaw in my novel.

I hope all this will serve to illustrate how every aspect of your life can be regarded as research for your novel. Life itself is one long process of research. Bad experiences and good, failures and humiliations: nothing is wasted, or lost. Surely this is the ultimate recycling! It is certainly one of the things I most love about fiction writing.

4 WHAT'S CREATIVE WRITING? TIPS FOR NEW WRITERS

Creative writing starts with passion. Therefore, if you want to be a creative writer, the first thing to do is identify your passion. Then write out of your passion. But how? Is what you have to say best suited to poetry, short story, non-fiction article or novel? Your next step is to ask yourself what you love to read. Whatever it is – that's what you could start to write.

Let's say you want to start writing a novel. Think of a phrase that's the perfect title for a book. That could be your starting point. And so now you are on a new threshold.

We can learn a lot from our ancestors. For instance, if you visit the Museum of London's prehistoric galleries, you'll find that Bronze Age people would build their roundhouses with the entrance facing the midwinter solstice. They would then consult their ancestors before making an offering to the new threshold. Now, perhaps modern builders have a comparable ritual – I don't know. But if they don't – perhaps they should. And so should those embarking on a long-term building project like a novel. I love the idea of 'making an offering to a new threshold'. And what I have to say here is like an offering to the new threshold.

First, where do your ideas come from? From life itself, all around you, wherever you are. Ideas fly past, and you catch them. Listen to conversations in every situation. Observe people. Eavesdrop in waiting rooms, cafes, offices and restaurants, or on trains and buses. Don't forget to have a notebook with you at all times – and keep notes. And, if you have a notebook system, you'll need to build in time to review your notebooks and retrieve your ideas.

Then you have to apply the following secrets of writing:

1. **Avoid not writing.** Take your craft seriously; believe that what you're doing is of sufficient value that you are going to carve out time for it. Book time for it if necessary – put it in your diary. Get in there and do it. Don't be afraid of the blank screen or blank page.

2. **Pay attention to structure.** Break down the book in your head into an outline. You could do it on a piece of software like Scrivener, or you could do it through a wall of Post-it Notes, or you could plot it on a storyboard; or you could write your novel as a short story first. But realise that you are unique and may have your own special way of working that is right for you. With a novel, sometimes writers find they can't plot too far ahead (though be aware you may have to go back and

impose structure later). If that is the case for you:

3. **Go on the journey and see what happens.** If a character develops a life of his or her own, it's a good sign. Some say the characters create the plot. Keep asking why, what, where, how, when.

4. **Set yourself a goal.** Try for a thousand words per working day, if you respond well to deadlines and schedules. If not write anyway.

5. **Don't talk your novel out of existence.** Write that first draft. I believe it's not a good idea to discuss the details of your novel with anyone until you've written it. Then you can seek feedback, and redraft, and revise and revise and revise.

Finally, when your book is finished to the very best of your ability and beyond, send it off to literary agents. And be prepared for rejection. Remember – you write because you are compelled to, because you cannot 'not write'. Take note of these wise words from popular author Adrian Plass: 'If things fall apart, pick up the pieces and carry on. Don't despair. There are strange things going on behind the scenes.'

5 ELEMENTS THAT MAKE UP A GOOD FICTION STORY

I believe in the power of story. And, of course, in various cultures story-tellers have held power; in Celtic communities, for instance, the Bard was second only to the Chief; consider the fact that the layout of a Bronze Age home gravitated around the centre where an elaborate chair was placed for the story-teller; and witness the strength of the oral tradition, out of which Homer came with his tales of the Trojan war, and of the journeys of Odysseus.

Given that the secular gods of this society are celebrity and fame and wealth, it is hardly surprising that the story-tellers have found themselves drawn in. And, thus, you have the cult of the celebrity bestselling novelist. Yes, sometimes our culture rewards a story-teller – but it is very uneven in the way it spreads its blessing. And, beyond every famous successful writer, there stand many others who are faithfully doing exactly the same thing – crafting stories.

So what are the elements of a good fiction story? Here are the five elements I believe are absolutely essential:

1. **Characters that catch the reader's imagination.** As in reality, so in fiction stories, individuals have a private and a public life. And it's the private life that yields the stories by which they live. Especially for a fiction writer, you cannot afford to present someone solely by how they behave in community, as they appear to other people. To me, the joy of fiction is that you are inside the characters, you feel how they feel: you experience life through their eyes, through their minds and hearts. We all have bright and dark areas in our characters. Our lives are a process of facing down our demons – archetypal story structure often includes dual characters like Spiderman and Peter Parker, or Superman and Clark Kent. Both these superheroes battle with the duality of dark and light in their characters. On one side is the bold, brilliant, public face; on the other side we find the quiet, the obscure, the vulnerable.

2. **Archetypal theme.** No matter how light you think your story is, the fact remains, that in order to give the reader a strong experience, ultimately there has to be an archetypal theme behind it. This can be friendship, loyalty, love, betrayal, loss, redemption, grief, despair, fear – but all of these are archetypal, meaning they are profoundly part of human experience. The story can be light, humorous, hard-

boiled, playful, serious, panoramic or any one of a number of different styles; but there will be an archetypal theme behind it. And then all is down to the author, as to which angle to take. Any originality a story has lies in the angle that the author takes.

3. **Emotional charge.** Every successful story, even if it is pared-down in style, and doesn't ever describe the characters' feelings, as in Neil Gaiman's *Coraline*, or John Fowles' *The Collector*, carries its own emotional charge. This can come from the author's selection of events, and once again the angle the author chooses to take; the information the author decides to use, and the information the author keeps out of sight. If the story elicits a strong response from the reader, that story inevitably has 'emotional charge'.

4. **Unexpected turning point.** Whether a story is a suspense, or a thriller, or a mystery, or any other genre, a powerful turning point is key. Of course this plays its part within classic story-structure. This is why Daphne du Maurier's *Rebecca* is so universally loved. The turning point shocks. This has a lot to do with what is hidden from us, and what is revealed, during the progress of the story. The skilful withholding of information, the subtle drip-feeding of clues: all this plays

its part in determining the effect that turning point will have on us.

5. **X Factor.** This is the final, unknown element, which cannot be discounted. It evades the teachers of creative writing courses, the writers of 'how-to' books; but it is there, undeniable. It has to do with the spirit behind the novel, and the spirit of the age in which the author writes, and the age in which the story is received. In Jane Austen's apparently simple romance novel about love, sex and money, *Pride and Prejudice*, we can analyse – and many have – but where exactly do we locate the X factor? Yet it is there, mysterious, elusive, mercurial. Stories with X factor have characters who haunt us, dilemmas we can relate to in every generation. Thomas Hardy's novel *The Mayor of Casterbridge* touches a deep nerve in human experience. You cannot chase X factor. You have to work with your unconscious, be true to yourself, and let go.

I have loved many books in my life, but the ones that stand out for me have all the above five elements. Some have the power to shock and electrify the reader: authors such as Joseph Conrad, Graham Greene and Shusaku Endo. Others have characters that haunt you through the years: Jane Eyre and Mr Rochester, Cathy and Heathcliffe, Lizzy Bennett and Darcy, Pip and

Estella; perhaps Bathsheba from Thomas Hardy's *Far From the Madding Crowd* or Raskolnikov in Dostoyevsky's *Crime and Punishment*, or Oscar Wilde's *The Portrait of Dorian Gray*; or the master-criminal Count Fosco in Wilkie Collins' *The Woman in White*, or maybe Dorothea in George Eliot's *Middlemarch*, or Nicholas Darrow in Susan Howatch's *Mystical Paths*.

And I also favour authors who are witty, perceptive and brilliantly funny – like PG Wodehouse, Tom Sharpe, David Lodge, Jerome K Jerome, Dodie Smith, Stella Gibbons and Jilly Cooper. I respond to authors whose work shows warmth and compassion, such as Katie Fforde and Joanna Trollope, or those who sail to the furthest reaches of the human psyche, such as Iris Murdoch or Susan Howatch. And among my most-loved books are those which tell of a small person harnessing the power of loyalty, friendship and love to overcome great odds – JK. Rowling's *Harry Potter* stories, Tolkien's *The Lord of the Rings*, or CS. Lewis's *The Lion, the Witch and the Wardrobe*. I have marvelled, too, at the imaginative fireworks in Philip Pullman's *His Dark Materials* trilogy.

6 THREE TIPS FOR CREATING A WORK OF REALISTIC FICTION

I chose this title because the word 'realistic' is so open to abuse and misunderstanding. For the purposes of this chapter in relation to writing fiction, let us begin by defining 'realistic'. I take the word to mean not only 'set in, and dealing, with, the world which we all experience in our daily lives' but also 'convincing and recognisable from our own experience'. Achieving realism in fiction is one of the paradoxes which I most enjoy as a creative writer.

1. Start by reminding yourself of a well-known phrase, which is almost a cliché of real life; for example, **There are always two sides to every story**. The first requirement of 'realistic' fiction is that the characters are believable. In other words, the reader recognises them from somewhere in his or her own experience, and says, whether unconsciously or not, "Yes. Real people are like this." You may happen to believe that with some people, 'what you see is what you get'; but no fiction writer can afford to present characters of whom this is true. My own

view is that in 'real' life, we can never fathom all the deep motivations and drivers behind the personalities of others; as often as not, it's difficult enough to honestly identify and face our own. The psychologist Carl Jung was very aware of this when he described the principle of 'the shadow', the dark side of ourselves which we project onto others and are most ready to criticise or fear when we see it 'out there'. Writers who fully meet the challenge of this in their fiction are those who create the most 'realistic' characters. For 'realistic' perhaps we can also use the word 'truthful'. And those who read psychological thriller fiction, at least, want to know what's going on beneath the surface. The truth lies through and behind the complex, strange and subtle.

2. Then consider all the limitations and conditions of the 'real' world of the senses that surrounds us every day. This can be a very enjoyable challenge for realistic fiction writers; just as much so as for those who write fantasy fiction, who still need to **create a world with consistent rules and laws**. A creative writer can have fun with this simply because the role of a novelist is in itself an impossible one. We play God, as a novelist; certainly not a privilege any of us can enjoy in real life. It may even be why we become fiction

writers in the first place; perhaps we are all failed megalomaniacs, and the fictional world is the only world over which we can have meaningful control. But we have to respect and acknowledge the limitations of the senses, and ensure that our godlike status as a novelist never compromises the laws of real life.

3. **Be aware** though of a very strange and almost sinister fact, which gives the lie to the word 'realistic': art imitates life, doesn't it? Or can it be true, as Oscar Wilde suggests in his 1889 essay, *The Decay of Lying,* that **life imitates art**? Because I have come to treat this seriously. Be careful what you create from your imagination; real life can sometimes start to imitate it. Not that I am suggesting, of course, that Thomas Harris went roaming round in his Hannibal Lecter persona having created *Silence of the Lambs*; but just hold in your mind that, even in real life, strange things can go on behind the scenes.

7 UNIVERSAL THEMES IN FICTION

Powerful universal themes in fiction usually remain undiscerned by the author, until he or she comes to look over the manuscript of the novel for a substantive edit. Story is all about people interacting with each other, and how they handle their conflicting desires. The theme can often be within the unconscious of the author, and therefore not something that can be contrived when planning the novel.

An alternative way of expressing 'theme' is 'controlling idea'. As Robert McKee says in his book *Story,* 'the more beautifully you shape your work around' this theme or controlling idea, 'the more meanings audiences will discover' in your work as 'they take your idea and follow its implications into every aspect of their lives'.

Examples of powerful universal themes are: spiritual searching, emotional needs, unfulfilled dreams, a thirst for truth, craving for intimacy, fear of death, lust for power.

A reader need never define the theme consciously in order to respond to it within a novel. We recognise a powerful story when it takes hold of us. The curious thing about themes is that very often different people can come up with very different ways of identifying the themes in a work of fiction. This again is an indication of the greatness of a novel. And then, of course, the identification of themes in great literature can be an arduous task for schoolchildren and English Literature GCSE students; and this very task can sometimes be responsible for putting them off the novels in question. A survey of some of my favourite novels of all time comes up with these themes:

Joseph Conrad: *Heart of Darkness* – conflict between reality and darkness

Graham Greene: *The End of the Affair* – hatred of self; love and hate of God

Charlotte Bronte: *Jane Eyre* – clash between conscience and passion; search for sense of belonging and love

Emily Bronte: *Wuthering Heights* – nature against civilisation; revenge and repetition; love and passion

Jane Austen: *Pride and Prejudice* – love, reputation and class

Charles Dickens: *Great Expectations* – crime, social class, ambition

Thomas Hardy: *Far From the Madding Crowd* – unrequited love

Dostoyevsky: *Crime and Punishment* – alienation from society

Oscar Wilde: *The Portrait of Dorian Gray* – aestheticism versus duplicity; supremacy of youth and beauty

Wilkie Collins: *The Woman in White* – substituted identity

JRR Tolkien: *The Lord of the Rings* – the

corrupting nature of power; death and immortality; self-sacrifice

Each one of these novels has several other themes as well. The universality of these themes is what makes these novels classic.

I believe authors achieve this kind of power in their stories by working with the limited freedom of movement in their own lives and trusting themselves to the unconscious.

8 STRATEGIES TO DEVELOP CREATIVE AND IMAGINATIVE WRITING

Creative writers feed their imaginations by observing and interacting with and receiving from the world. Impressions that come to us must be captured before any critical voice comes in. I find the cross-fertilisation of ideas between different art forms very important in creative writing. And that is why going to art exhibitions can be very helpful – and is the focus for this chapter.

When viewing art, we can be open not only to how the art work makes us feel, but also to the thoughts that spring into our minds without any conscious process. It's best to let go of any critical impulse and simply experience the art, and allow it to make impressions upon us. As a creative writer, the part this will all play in any story structure comes later, and sometimes much later – even perhaps several books later.

As an illustration of this, consider an exhibition I visited where all the artists had been inspired by lace. Their work showed me how holes, spaces and gaps concentrate meaning within themselves, through the creation of networks, connections, and boundaries. I saw an inverted crystal cathedral hanging from the ceiling, and a room filled with a disturbing and sinister network of black embroidery wool, enclosing four long white dresses. A glittering rose pattern punched on another wall of the gallery seemed to have been created with sequins, or glass beads, or crystals. But they were only holes. Behind them a large window let in natural light; and the holes defined the pattern.

I entered a room which plunged the viewer into darkness and only threads of light could be seen, curving around, above and through space, given meaning by the hole of darkness at the centre. In my imagination that hole could become the portal to another world.

Later, I thought of another analogy. When we write a novel often we don't necessarily know what our theme or controlling idea is, or indeed exactly how the main protagonist is going to live that out. But when we have completed the book, we know – or think we know. After the book is published, and in the hands of readers, a gap opens up – the gap between what we thought we meant, and what the reader will make of it. That can sometimes be very different indeed. There is space between us and our readers; but somehow the threads that enclose the space will create a connection.

So it is in story structure. Gaps are essential to great story: the gap that opens up between the expectation of the reader, and what actually happens. And from that gap pours a flood of insight.

9 HOW TO PICK A TOPIC TO WRITE CREATIVELY ABOUT

Creativity as a process has only one true source, across all fields of creative endeavour, whether that be in the arts or the sciences – and that is, the unconscious. Ayd Instone in *Creativity and the Beatles* has this to say:

> *It wasn't until 1995 that Paul McCartney realised that his 1965 song, 'Yesterday', apparently on the surface, about the loss of a lover was actually about the very real loss of his own mother a few years earlier from cancer...a pain that he wasn't consciously aware of when he wrote it. Perhaps creativity is a ghost after all, a spectre of energy, emotion and hidden memory that at certain times, perhaps when we least expect it, will come to haunt us.*

It is well known that the idea for the tune of 'Yesterday' first came to Paul McCartney in a dream. Dreams have a large part to play in how our unconscious minds communicate with us.

Whether we write, or whether we create in any other field, for the initial inspiration we are reliant on the unconscious. This can make us insecure and vulnerable; for control comes from the conscious mind, and the unconscious lies beyond. Of course, there's a time when structure and reason are vital; but my point here is that when you pick your topic to write creatively about, behind all your conscious selections there will be something else at work that you can have no control over at all.

And many great novels which catch the imagination of large readerships have been based on ideas that arose from the author's unconscious. Take for instance the story of *Dr Jekyll and Mr Hyde*. These characters came to Robert Louis Stevenson in a dream. And the novelist John Fowles has said that the first idea for *The French Lieutenant's Woman* came to him simply through an image of a woman standing alone at the end of the Cobb at Lyme Regis, gazing out to sea. He didn't know where the image had come from. But there it was – and a novel arose from it. And creativity is not confined to the arts. Scientists too are creative. Thomas Edison said many of his most brilliant ideas and insights came to him in his 'creative alpha state' between wakefulness and sleep.

Therefore, I believe the answer to the challenge of 'How to pick a topic to write creatively about' lies in your unconscious mind. This is the key to the creative process.

10 HOW TO KNOW WHICH POINT OF VIEW TO USE IN A STORY

It has been said that there's no original plot or story around. But what makes any story unique is the angle the author takes. And the angle is determined by the point of view (POV). Choosing the best point of view is absolutely critical to the success of a story. It takes great skill to write a successful novel from the point of view of a character who is peripheral to the central drama. Certainly if it's taken from the point of view of a character the reader doesn't care about much then the story will fail.

In selecting the best point of view, one determining factor stands out above all others – that is, high emotional stakes. When you look at your story you need to ask: "Whose story is this?" The answer lies in the person who has the highest emotional stakes in what is going on.

Making decisions on this is often more challenging than you may imagine. After all, a fictional story can often arise from the unconscious – which, as I'm sure Carl Jung, that master of the subject would agree, can be very undisciplined and chaotic. Once the story has been created, then some kind of rational structure must be forged for it. These are the five questions the author has to ask him or herself:

1. What is the central question of the story, to which the reader wants to know the answer?

2. What information must be held back, in order to create suspense?

3. What will the outcome of the story be – the answer to that central question?

4. Who has the most to gain or lose, hanging on the answer to the central question?

5. With whom will the reader most want to identify?

Sometimes, of course, a new story can spring up directly from the main POV character and their dilemma. In other cases, however, a story can arise from the unconscious mind, and then the author needs to do some excavation work, in order to extract from that story idea the individual who is most imperilled, emotionally or physically, from the working out of the plot.

It can be an entertaining exercise to imagine a famous story from the point of view of a different character. For instance, consider the *Harry Potter* stories taken from the point of view of Hermione or Ron – interesting, but not as powerful as the story from Harry's POV. Then consider the story from Snape's POV – disastrous! There would be no suspense whatsoever. Admittedly that is rather an extreme example.

And then, finally, we turn to examples which look on the surface like exceptions to my rule of high emotional stakes. Take the case of the new tenant at Wuthering Heights, who opens Emily Bronte's classic story. And then events are recounted by Nellie Dean, the housekeeper. So in what way can Nellie be described as the character who has the highest emotional stakes in the story? Perhaps *Wuthering Heights* is a special case. By virtue of Nellie's long service with this family, her devotion and sheer emotional stability, she becomes a pivotal point for the melodramatic tale of tumultuous emotions, violence and tragedy. Perhaps then, 'mental and emotional stability' might be another qualification for a POV character, especially in a tale such as this – in other words, the one character with whom your reader will want to identify – if only on grounds of sanity.

11 FIVE TIPS ON HOW TO MAKE YOUR FICTIONAL CHARACTERS ENGAGING

So you've begun your novel and perhaps you've already had lots of ideas for your characters. They will probably be a composite of different people you've met in the past, or even different aspects of yourself. But how do you make them engaging? And not just the main protagonist, but all the principal characters? And dare I say it, even the antagonist or villain? Because no one is completely good or completely bad; and, for a villain to be truly convincing, there must be some elements of the character which the reader can either recognise, relate to, or even empathise with – yes, even Gollum and Voldemort!

The same things that make you like people in real life are the things which make fictional characters engaging. We don't like people who are self-appointed; people who are hard and impregnable; people who are (or appear to be) boring and predictable, and people who refuse to ever freely share anything about themselves with anybody else.

To make things simpler, when I refer to 'the hero' I also mean 'heroine'.

So here's how to make your fictional characters engaging (from my own experience):

1. **Your character must not be self-appointed.** This means that, if you want your reader to like the hero, that hero must not appoint himself to the task he ends up doing, or the quest which he ends up fulfilling. Before the hero sets out on the quest, he must have been tested, and changed; he must have died (to his default expectations of himself) and been reborn; and he only takes on the quest because he is tested again and again, and succeeds. He does not set out on the quest because he thinks he's good and big and clever enough to do it.

2. **Your character needs to show vulnerability.** This is vital. We cannot like people who are hard and impregnable. Even Gollum touches our hearts. He was once a warm, sensitive being – but he risks being destroyed by lust for the Ring. Frodo chooses to believe Gollum can be redeemed. (And actually, he can; but he ultimately chooses not to be).

3. **You must explore your character inside and outside. The reader must be intrigued by the gap between what the character says of himself, and what other characters say of him.** Very few of us have one hundred per cent self-knowledge, and if we did, we probably wouldn't be likeable. The same principle

applies to the gap between what the character says or thinks of himself, and what he actually does.

4. **You must know your character's backstory.** What happened before he came to enter this story? Why? How? Where? When? What is his motivation?

5. **You must defeat the reader's expectations, and your own.** In real life we can never truly fathom each other. This is the joy of writing fiction, in which the author can play God. You can let the reader into the inmost hearts of your characters, if you choose. And yet, you must always defeat the reader's expectations. Defeat your own too. That's when your characters become as real as they can be, in fiction. That is where inspiration, intuition and originality lie. And that comes from the unconscious mind – as anyone who has studied the writings of Carl Jung will know.

12 HOW TO CREATE A NOVEL THAT YOUR READERS WON'T WANT TO PUT DOWN

There are five essential things you as an author must do if you want to create a novel that your reader won't want to put down: 1. **create empathy with the main character** and their quest; 2. **captivate the reader with your tone of voice** 3. **engage the reader's emotions** 4. **keep questions open** and 5. **build up suspense**.

First, though, you must remember that only a proportion of all fiction readers actually want a novel they can't put down. Some readers like a novel that has a gentle pace that can indeed be put down, to fit in with their lifestyle, and can then be taken up some time later and the story picked up again without the reader having to go back and remind themselves who certain characters are and how they relate to each other. This in itself is a skill to be admired. But here we are talking about the kind of novel which has its audience hooked from page one, in such a way that engagement with the story is absolute.

1. **Empathy with the main character and his or her quest.** The reader's attention will be lost unless strong feelings are aroused about the chief protagonist and the

central question of the novel. Of course this varies through different genres; and the reader of hard-boiled crime fiction probably won't talk in terms of 'feelings' at all, but nevertheless there will be a powerful urge to continue reading, to care about what happens and to want to know the answers to the questions the author poses.

2. **Captivate the reader with your tone of voice.** A captivating tone of voice comes from the narration and from the main viewpoint character – there are many errors to be made here; if a reader feels patronised, fed too much information, or antagonised by the voice of the novel, nothing can more swiftly guarantee that they will give up on the story.

3. **Engage the reader's emotions.** The reason why a reader cannot put a novel down is also a great deal to do with the emotional stakes – do we fear for the main character; do we hope for them; how strongly do we care about the outcome?

4. **Keep questions open and structure the supply of answers.** Within classic story structure there must be one central over-arching question which is kept open throughout the course of the novel; and when that question is answered, the story is over. But beneath that question many

others must be set, belonging to the sub-plots; and when answers are provided to these subsidiary questions, they must lead to others, and so on.

5. **Build up suspense.** This involves the careful selection of information, and critical decisions about what can be revealed to the reader, when; and what has to be withheld until later. A writer must exercise skill, fine judgement and instinct in this. Another essential aspect of suspense has to do with viewpoint – what does each character know? It is vital that an author keeps strong control of this, and it is an area where mistakes can easily be made.

A truly unputdownable novel can make life rather difficult for a reader – you must have that open novel in your hand on the bus or train, whilst you are cooking, late at night in bed, even walking along the street. But making this happen can be great fun for a writer, and experiencing it is one of the greatest joys of being a keen reader of fiction. All readers can find ways of coping with it within their lifestyle – I certainly can!

13 THE WRITING PROCESS FOR CREATING A NOVEL IN LESS THAN A MONTH

This title was inspired by the popular website NaNoWriMo (National Novel Writing Month). NaNoWriMo is held every year in November, the purpose being to encourage writers to complete a project; and the task is: write a novel of at least 50,000 words in a month.

By the word 'novel' we must mean, of course, 'the first draft of a novel'. I completed the first draft of my paranormal thriller, *A Passionate Spirit,* using these techniques.

Here are three tips to have that completed first draft of a novel in a month:

1. **Do your preparation work before the month begins**. Ideas will have been hatching in your mind for the last couple of years, perhaps; and now you have a ground plan. You have created a one-sentence storyline, and expanded it to a blurb and a synopsis and perhaps you have drawn up a list of scenes for your novel. Not everybody needs to have done this before they begin writing the novel. Some like to plunge into the writing with

two or three characters and a conflict in mind, and let the story emerge. But I had already been thinking about my characters for a year or so before beginning my novel. And I know from experience what it's like to allow your characters to take over. Characters will do that anyway, even if you have a plan. But I now believe having a plan is a very good way to start, even if the plan is radically changed by the time you've finished your first draft.

2. **Begin writing, and don't go back to edit**. Control your desire to look over previous chapters and assess or improve them. This needs great discipline. Just keep writing even if you suspect what you are writing is rubbish, because you are going to go back over your manuscript anyway after the month is up and use it as the basis for your second draft.

3. **Don't fall into the trap of slacking or subsiding or falling away because your novel feels as if it's sinking in the middle**. Introduce something crazy or bizarre that occurs to you; just follow that instinct, introduce it into your plot, set your characters the task of dealing with it and keep on writing.

Those who find their minds go blank at the prospect of producing a full-length work of the imagination should remember this one thing: creating a first draft of fiction requires only motivation and courage. It requires you to forget everything negative you ever believed of yourself, and to believe in whatever ideas come to you, believe in them enough to incorporate them in your first draft. When you read your manuscript through in a month's time, you may be amazed at what you came up with, apparently 'out of nowhere'.

14 HOW TO START A NOVEL

The beginning of a book must have some kind of emotional charge. It has to hook the reader in the first paragraph or first page. In the case of a novel the best way to start is with a scene of conflict in the life of your main protagonist. This scene needs to show where your main protagonist currently is, in his or her life, and what the tensions are in his or her situation.

One of the courses I took a few years ago covered story structure in terms of the seven point arc. I remember it mentioned that you begin a story with *stasis* – in other words, where the MP is right now. Then there is an *inciting event* – in classic story structure of myth and legend, the MP receives a call, which will move him or her out of the ordinary world, into a new world. The MP can either accept this call or reject it. Either way it is the invitation to a quest. There are many ways of illustrating story structure, using different metaphors but the format described above corresponds to 'the hero's journey', which I have found very helpful. By looking at the story structure of, say *The Wizard of Oz*, or any other popular fairy tale, myth or legend, you see the main character setting out upon a quest; and the principles of what follows may be applied across the construction of every story. It makes big sense to me.

Many novelists find one of the trickiest things is to

know where to start your story. Finding out that key moment is a great challenge. You may not discover it until you've written the whole book. I would advise the aspiring writer not to worry about it too much, but to write the book all the way through first; because, inevitably, you will go back to the beginning and probably rewrite it several times. You can often only find out where your story starts, that moment of tension, after you have written the story.

Sometimes the story may start three chapters later than you thought it did, and you will need to cut out your first chapters entirely. Or maybe it starts further back. Either way, it can be very exciting and revealing, when you find that perfect point where your story starts.

15 HOW TO FICTIONALISE CHARACTERS

It is tempting for an author to use real people as characters in novels. But the best characterisation comes from a blend of personal observation and imagination. A fictional creation should be just that. A principal character cannot truly convince the reader unless the author fully inhabits the character, mind, body and spirit; and that can only be done through the power of imaginative sympathy. In this chapter I also argue that this power is fed by a knowledge and understanding of psychology.

In response to his observation of human experience and behaviour, Carl Jung postulated the theory of the 'collective unconscious'. This collects and organises personal experiences in a similar way with each member of the species. We may see this operating in the world of creative writing when millions of us respond in a similar positive way to particular characters or relationships, for instance Elizabeth Bennett and Mr Darcy in Jane Austen's *Pride and Prejudice*. We can then say that the story touches upon areas of human experience which are universal.

Quantum theory suggests that we humans have free will but are limited in what we do; using the analogy of a chess game, each piece has a limited freedom of movement. We are not aware of the existence of the laws which influence our every action, and each individual is limited in a unique way. Tolstoy understood this when he wrote in *War and Peace*: 'we must renounce a freedom that does not exist and recognise a dependence of which we are not conscious.'

How can we see this working out in some well-known stories? Let me suggest a few examples from my own fiction reading.

1. **A desire for truth.** This is the central issue in Orwell's novel *1984*; Winston Smith's struggle to undermine the Party's monopoly on Truth has struck a deep chord with so many.

2. **A longing for intimacy.** Emma Donoghue drew upon this for the high emotional stakes in her novel *Room* as we witnessed an extraordinary level of spiritual and psychological intimacy between the five-year old boy narrator and his mother during their imprisonment, an intimacy broken after their escape from captivity.

3. **Fear of death or the unknown.** We find a preoccupation with this in the *Harry Potter* stories and it comes out repeatedly in the character of Harry. JK Rowling said she could never have written the *Harry Potter* books if it wasn't for the fact that she loved her mother, and her mother died. Albus Dumbledore often speaks to Harry

about death, throughout the stories. "It is the unknown we fear when we look upon death and darkness, nothing more," he says to Harry.

I believe authors fictionalise characters by letting go of the need to 'copy', 'represent real life' or 'get the facts right', and instead trusting to their unconscious to process observation, imagination and knowledge.

16 HOW TO DEVELOP A CHARACTER USING COMPLEXES

I believe that to create a fictional character with power and authenticity, the author needs a basic understanding of psychology. That can, of course, come through the process of living, and through a long-established habit of observing people: and not necessarily through study. In this chapter, however, I suggest a knowledge of Jungian psychological concepts is useful; and to illustrate this, I'll take the example of *complexes*.

A complex, as developed in the writings of Carl Jung, may be defined as 'a core pattern of emotions, memories, perceptions and wishes in the personal unconscious organised around a common theme such as power or status'. The notion of a *complex* may even be misused in common speech: we may too readily hear of someone described as having an inferiority / guilt / martyr complex. But this can be fruitful for a creative writer; though it has to be handled with care.

1. An **inferiority complex** may lead your character to interpret everything in the light of this set of notions: "I'm not good enough", "my opinions don't count" or "I'm afraid to put myself forward". Take PG Wodehouse as an example; see *Jeeves*

and The Inferiority Complex of Old Sippy among numerous other stories. Here we often meet shy young men attempting to battle those who are louder, bigger, better-looking, and more self-confident, to win the girl they love.

2. Often, whether a fictional character displays a certain complex can be a matter of interpretation by the reader. I suggest a **martyr complex** may lie behind the outlook and actions of Thomas Hardy's *Tess of the D'Urbervilles*. Tess behaves like a martyr sacrificing herself. Many readers may feel Tess casts herself in the role of victim.

3. The **guilt complex** is used extensively in Dostoyevsky's *The Brothers Karamazov*. Several characters experience intense guilt; but the exception to this is Smerdyakov who murders Fyodor yet does not blame himself; though he's the only character technically guilty, he feels the least liability for it. Thus the author sheds light on some of his own religious questions and doubts.

4. The **power complex** may operate where someone is at the top of a hierarchical structure. Take, for example, the pitiless schoolmaster, Thomas Gradgrind, in Dickens' *Hard Times;* he uses his power over his young pupils to fill them with

facts and to stamp out all colour, adventure and magic from their lives; or even Aunt Reed in Charlotte Bronte's *Jane Eyre*, as she exercises what little power she finds in her own life over her vulnerable young niece.

So there's plenty of inspiration here for you as you develop characters in your novel who will inspire love, pity, fury, fascinated horror, or even self-searching in your reader. But take care: not too many characters with complexes, please (unless you are a novelist of genius like Dostoyevsky). These characters must be balanced with at least one person who is calm and centred – in the interests of giving your novel authenticity!

17 HOW TO CREATE LAYERS WITHIN EACH OF YOUR CHARACTERS

Every person consists of several layers, starting with the thin veneer you see on the surface, then tooling down deeper and deeper to the core which remains hidden to many. But a novelist's task is to penetrate these layers. This must be one of the most enjoyable challenges in fiction writing: building up a character in layers, through what they say of themselves, what others say of them, through their actions and words, through thoughts, hopes and dreams, through references to former events and relationships. And the task which is most difficult and testing yet carries the most excitement is knowing what to reveal, how much and when. The fiction writer uses real life as a springboard, and then plunges into the water, passing through the shallows, into the depths of character creation.

1. When your observations of life have brought you to the stage at which you are ready to start creating a character, first you must **write a character bible**. You will refer to this throughout your novel, and it will contain a large amount of information you will never explicitly use within the story. But it's vital you know all

these things about your character. Here you'll make notes on your character's values, ambition, goal, conflict and so on. But you will also need to record such details as date of birth, colour of hair and eyes, weight, height, work history, family background, etc. Here too you can record the character's philosophy of life, best childhood memory, and a synopsis of the novel as if it were taken from this character's point of view.

2. Once you have your character bible for each character, and have planned your scenes (or if you prefer simply have a rough idea of the direction the story may take) then you can **write the first draft of the novel**. The magic begins when the characters start taking over and determining how the plot will change and twist, in a way that can totally surprise the author.

3. When you have your first draft, you will then go back and look over this canvas that you have filled with paint, and **start focussing on the details**. Then you will find the anomalies, the logical impossibilities, the inaccuracies. None of that mattered in the first draft because you were simply covering the canvas. But it is at this point that you will go much more deeply into the layering of your characters, and will acknowledge things about them

that may mean you have to alter what you wrote in your character bible.

4. It is when you reach the point of **offering your novel for professional appraisal and feedback**, that you first experience the miracle. This is when people talk to you about your characters, taking them seriously as if they were real living beings with a separate existence and integrity of their own. It makes all the isolation and stubbornness and obsession of being a novelist worthwhile. The next step is, of course, a contract of publication, and then beyond that your readers, the audience you always wanted to connect with.

Great fictional characters do indeed have a life of their own, because then they inhabit people's minds and imaginations, and are carried through the years, like Elizabeth Bennett, or Miss Haversham, or Oliver Twist, or Jane Eyre, or, perhaps, Hercule Poirot, or James Bond, or Harry Potter.

These are the heights, but it is no business of the novelist to even think of them while creating and layering the character. How your characters and story will be received is irrelevant at that point. Only the act of creation itself matters.

18 HOW TO CREATE VILLAINOUS CHARACTERISTIC TRAITS IN YOUR WRITING

An effective fictional villain has, to my mind, one essential characteristic. The villain should build up in the reader a passionate desire for his or her comeuppance. If the novel ends without one, or the villain is allowed to triumph, that makes for a profound sense of dissatisfaction in the reader.

So how do you as the fiction writer build up this strong emotional reaction in your reader? Fundamentally, you need to show the main protagonist, your hero, striving to attain the story goal, and constantly being undermined or threatened or endangered by the subtle, invidious workings of the villain. Within classic story structure, this kind of subtle hostility then builds up to violent attack, death traps, and the blackest of black moments for the hero.

A villain is one who exploits, manipulates, betrays. A villain is utterly self-seeking, wreaks havoc in the lives of others, and destroys without pity. But a villain may take the form of a hostile environment; adverse political or economic circumstances; a psychological state; or an inner demon. Your villain may appear as a pious, moaning, self-appointed martyr; or a religious hypocrite (the Bronte sisters excelled in portraying those); the true villain can be not the one who actually does the evil, but the one who lurks in the background creating the conditions for the evil to germinate and thrive and flourish. The joy of fiction is that this kind of villain may be brought out into the light, and be exposed. The tragedy of life is that this kind of villain often goes undiscovered and unpunished.

But we fiction writers often do ensure that our villains get their comeuppance. Charles Dickens sets up poetic justice for Fagin and Quilp; JK Rowling brings Lord Voldemort to his final downfall; Wilkie Collins arranges an ignominious end for his Napoleonic master-criminal Count Fosco. Of course there are the fiction writers who supply the exceptions that prove the rule. For Thomas Hardy, perhaps, the pitiless gods are the villains; they are the ones who bring Tess of the d'Urbervilles to a tragic end. And do they get their comeuppance? No. Nevertheless, Hardy brings all his novels to a satisfying conclusion; and there is much to be learned from a careful study of his outcomes.

Why does a tragic end satisfy us? We look at all the elements of this; and it turns out that there is a deep level of meaning present. What we abhor is a vacuum. We always seek meaning. Sometimes a story with a beginning, a middle and an end supplies that meaning in itself. And just seeing that pattern, recognising that meaning, can supply the same emotional response as the comeuppance of the villain.

19 THE IMPORTANCE OF CHOOSING WORDS CAREFULLY: YOUR AUDIENCE'S INTERPRETATION MATTERS

Creative writers care about their audience's interpretation. And language is their raw material. How they craft it is all-important. To demonstrate this, take the extreme opposite case of another user of language: a spokesman for a corrupt politician. Recently in my favourite radio news programme, I heard one of our senior current affairs journalists interview a spokesman for an African politician who was refusing to step down from power in a disputed election which took place five months before.

You would think that of all people, spokesmen for political leaders would be expert at choosing their words carefully, with their audience's interpretation in mind. But no. They have another objective entirely.

The format was predictable. The journalist asked him how he could insist that his boss had legitimately been voted back into power, when the consensus of all the most highly respected international organisations was that he hadn't. Meanwhile, thousands of people were dying, as this particular politician used brute force to stay in power. A very stark ethical question, you may say. The spokesman then ignored that ethical question and stuck to his narrow line instead. He mentioned an internal committee, his country's constitutional council, according to whose elaborate systems and procedures, he claimed his boss had won the election.

The journalist then said, "Forgive me, but this is going to be very confusing for many people listening who are not intimately familiar with the way your constitution works." What he meant, of course, was: I suggest you are trying to pull the wool over our eyes.

But what did the spokesman reply? "Precisely!" he said. "You don't understand the complexities. And that's why I regard this as an international conspiracy." And what he meant was: I am going to ignore the ethical issues and pretend they don't exist, because my boss is a dangerous man who will stop at nothing to hold onto power.

Nevertheless, despite the actual words used by the spokesman, I think it likely that all reasonable listeners would have understood the subscript instead.

When George Orwell created his concept of 'NewSpeak' he touched upon something that is at the heart of human conflict. The language you use, and your awareness of how your audience will hear it, is all-important. The spokesman for the tyrant doesn't care how the audience will interpret. Power enforced with brutality has its own language.

However, creative writers do care how the audience will interpret. The power story-tellers wield is a much more subtle one; rather than persuade with gun or terror, this power appeals to hearts and minds; and the interpretation and response is won freely.

20 CHARACTER CREATION: THE MOST INTERESTING FICTIONAL CHARACTERS OF ALL

The success and the longevity of a great novel do not lie entirely in the hands of its hero. Many of my favourite novels come with a surprise gift – the character who is most interesting of all, who is *not* the main protagonist. This is the character you wonder about later, the character that seems to step outside the story and comment on it, or the one whose dilemma is never really solved by the outcome of the plot. This character may be the one who highlights the theme by negating it.

Here are three strong examples:

1. **Mr Bennett in** *Pride and Prejudice*
   Mr Bennett is the character around whom the story problem – the entailment – is centred. Mr Bennett is the one who could have seen the family crisis coming, and who, as the head of the family, has the power to avert it – Lydia's elopement, which threatens to ruin the family. Mr Bennett is the one who allows himself the luxury of standing outside the story and commenting flippantly on it, as if the fate of his family had never hung on the

decisions he made. In the end, the family is saved, by good fortune operating through the characters of Lizzie and Darcy – and not by Mr Bennett fulfilling his duty. And yet he says, "And so Darcy did everything ... I shall offer to pay him tomorrow; he will rant and storm, about his love for you, and there will be an end to the matter." And near the end we again see Mr Bennett's delicious irony in this remark to Lizzie: "I admire all my three sons-in-law highly. Wickham, perhaps is my favourite; but I think I shall like *your* husband quite as well as Jane's."

2. Gollum in *The Lord of the Rings*

I find Gollum as a character no simple villain, but heartrending. He is the one who lingers with you for a long time afterwards. He is the one some of us in our most honest moments may be able to relate to. Gollum started out as an ordinary member of the river folk, but became consumed by his lust for the Ring. Thereafter, it is as if he has given over all his power to the very worst in himself. And yet he is offered redemption, by Frodo. Frodo uses his real name, Smeagol, to try and recall Gollum to a sense of who he once was. He demonstrates trust to Gollum. This indicates Gollum can be redeemed if he chooses. And there are moments when he comes close, moments when we pity him so much, and long for him to be redeemed. Yet Gollum's final choice, to grasp the Ring, brings about his own destruction, and that of the Ring itself.

3. **Mr Tumnus in** *The Lion, the Witch and the Wardrobe*

Mr Tumnus the Fawn is the character I think of first whenever I think of *The Lion, the Witch and the Wardrobe*. Loveable, pure, innocent, representing the natural world, the first inhabitant of Narnia whom Lucy meets, who offers her hospitality and friendship – yet it is Mr Tumnus who is prevailed upon to spy for the White Witch, and first alerts her to the presence in Narnia of a Daughter of Eve. And Mr Tumnus suffers for it. But ultimately he is redeemed.

So I hope these examples serve to demonstrate how your main character will not carry the full weight of the novel's success. And when your hero stands up to receive the accolades, he can truly say, "I would never have done this without ..." and then he can credit his supporting team – and among them, the most interesting character of all.

21 HOW TO STRUCTURE YOUR WRITING TO IMPROVE THE FLOW OF THE STORY

Reading a novel is like going on a journey down a river. Sometimes the water is smooth and calm, sometimes rough; occasionally you may find yourself in whitewater rapids; and ultimately it flows into the sea. If your boat gets ambushed by a rogue current and becomes snarled up among tree roots and rushes in a muddy backwater, that spoils your journey. A page-turning, exciting and fast-plotted read is reasonably easy to attain, up to a certain point; but where many inexperienced writers get caught out is overall structure.

It has been said that plot is character and character is plot. In regard to structure, the key is the main protagonist who in this chapter I will assume is male. We need to know his conscious desire; and if his unconscious desire conflicts with it, that takes precedence. The spine of the story is the energy of the main protagonist's desire. Everything is structured around that. When a novel is strangely unsatisfactory, I suggest that a failure to fully understand and apply these principles of structure is at the heart of the problem.

Recently I read a novel which was an exciting, fast-paced, well-plotted story, with issues and characters I cared about. As I turned the pages, I found it gripping, and was planning to give it five stars. However, when I reached the final third of the novel, I realised I was going to have to downgrade it to four stars. I began to feel cheated, disappointed, short-changed. That is a sure sign the writer's problem lay in the structure. Here are three pointers, enabling you as a writer to explore this:

1. **Who is the main protagonist?**

There was some doubt about who the main protagonist was because the author moved from viewpoint to viewpoint so much. I began to feel I wanted more exploration of the MP's motivations and character. Some of his behaviour was that of a villain, not a hero. I wanted to understand and to be enabled to feel there were some redeeming factors.

2. **Character motivation**

A major female character, compassionate, caring, intelligent, was behaving in a way I just did not find believable in the circumstances. Why was she set on a course which might have terrible repercussions for her? What was there in her background that led her to behave as she did? The author had not explored this at all, he simply presented her behaviour.

3. **The main antagonist**

This was a 'mysterious enemy'. Our hero had started to guess the existence of this enemy but there was no build-up or gradual unravelling of information, through the technique of foreshadowing. Instead, the enemy was unexpectedly revealed in the final scene of the novel. Why? This strand of the story lacked progression. The unmasking and final defeat of the enemy, needs to be through the efforts and the personal resources and the striving of the main protagonist.

These three pointers will show you how critical character and motivation is to structure. Understand structure and apply its principles if you want to create a novel which flows well, like a journey down a great river.

22 HOW TO GET OVER WRITER'S BLOCK WHEN HALFWAY THROUGH YOUR NOVEL

My initial suggestion is this: write the first draft of your novel in a relatively short concentrated space of time. I suggest six weeks maximum. From my experience, you make yourself vulnerable to writer's block if you take too long to complete that first draft. Easy to say so, you may respond; what if the writing of your novel must be fitted in around a full-time job? What if there are many interruptions, and it's difficult to keep up the momentum of writing? The only answer to that is if you care about writing your novel, you will find the time. You will prioritise and remove distractions from your life.

Writer's block, from my own experience, is what happens when you lose passion and excitement and engagement with your characters. Suddenly you don't care anymore. Suddenly they no longer inspire you. I have come to realise there are a number of causes of this:

1. **You have an erratic writing schedule**, and you allow long spaces of time to elapse between writing sessions. The habit of discipline should train both mind and body; the mental powers of imagination,

observation, research, and concentration, allied to the body that sits at the table or desk, the hand that holds the pen and writes, or taps the keys of the laptop.

2. **You have not planned your novel beforehand**. I can recommend designing your novel using Snowflake Pro, novel design software created by Randy Ingermanson, who has (with Peter Economy) also written an excellent book on fiction writing. If you follow this guidance, you stand a good chance of avoiding writer's block. If you start by establishing structure, and move out to the details, then you are working from a stable position. It is like seeing the wood for the trees. If you know what your three Acts are, and you have already planned your major disasters: the first at the end of Act 1, the second in the middle of Act 2, and the third at the end of Act 2, then you will avoid what Ingermanson calls 'the flabby middle'. This is the zone where you will encounter writer's block, unless you have paid attention to structure.

3. **A character is failing to live up to his or her promise**. Then be bold and strike out... and ask "what if?" and go with whatever crazy idea first strikes you. Allow somebody new and unexpected to enter. Perhaps move your character to another setting, present the character with

an unforeseen challenge. Of course an over-proliferation of characters and locations is another danger. But this is your first draft. You can fix it later, can't you? And it's better than giving in to writer's block.

4. **The heart and soul have gone out of your novel**. You've designed your story, listed all your scenes, you've deleted some and moved others around, and you read through again and suddenly you realise the novel has become vacuous and empty. Writer's block can strike then too. But it needn't. Perhaps take a break from the writing, go out for a long walk or visit an art gallery or do something completely different that doesn't involve words, then come back to it afresh. Read through your scene list again and then your intuition may once again start to piece things together, make sense of it all.

5. **Your novel really isn't working**. There's nothing you can do to rescue it. If this is the case, then put it out of its misery, let it go, rest awhile and start to construct a new one. Never give up. Carry on writing. Your next novel is just around the corner.

23 GOOD THINGS TO DO TO IMPROVE YOUR CREATIVE WRITING

A creative writer can benefit from studying work in other fields of creativity. In this chapter I take as a role model a contemporary artist whose vibrant works not only uplift and enthral, but also give several insights for creative writers. Here are five highlights from the art of David Hockney (gathered together for his exhibition 'A Bigger Picture' at London's Royal Academy).

1. **Working from memory frees the imagination.** Hockney does a charcoal sketch in situ, then paints in studio; or he observes a landscape, then paints it from memory; or he paints wholly from his imagination. Working from memory sets the imagination free. This may be applied to the work of a novelist; a story which is over-reliant on research may teach the reader a lot but will it haunt the imagination for years?

2. **Notice the changes in one subject over time.** Hockney went back again and again to exactly the same fixed position in Woldgate Wood, East Yorkshire. He

painted the wood in May, July, October and November – each time capturing a different spirit. The same place – transformed over time. Here is an essential task of the creative writer; to show the changes in one protagonist made by varying pressures of time and plot and circumstance.

3. **Be alert to seize the opportunity that will quickly vanish.** Hawthorn blossom appears overnight and can disappear in one downpour of rain. Hockney was alert to the moment the blossom would appear. He called it 'action week'. He would instantly be out to paint with urgency. So must story-writers capture the opportunity that the creative imagination presents – whether that be a thought that comes during the night or on a long train journey, or in any other solitary moment. It must be captured with urgency or it will vanish.

4. **Focus intense concentration on one well-defined area.** Hockney filmed the landscape through nine cameras mounted on a grid on the front of his jeep as it moved slowly along. Each frame makes the viewer see the whole differently, by focussing intensely on the details within that frame – helping us to see as an artist sees. This is what a great novelist does in exploring the psyche of one character

who touches the spirit of the age.

5. **Harness the power of rediscovery.**

Hockney came back to the environment of his childhood, having spent many years away from it, living in California. Separation from a loved landscape only serves to feed the mind as it imagines and reflects. This is so in creative writing too. If you spend much time apart from something you can now only apprehend through memories, dreams, reflections, your expression of this in any art form will have much greater depth and intensity.

24 HOW TO SUCCESSFULLY WRITE
THE PLOT OF YOUR NOVEL
IN REVERSE

How can one write a good fiction story in reverse? This may seem a trick question until you realise this simple fact: a novel is defined by its outcome. Put it another way; every story has a 'controlling idea'; and this idea is embedded in the final climax of the story. You cannot know what you are really trying to say until you have your controlling idea. And the corollary of that is: you often cannot be sure what your controlling idea is until you've written your story. So what do you do?

1. Do your thinking, your wondering, your research, perhaps even write a plan – just a way to trick the unconscious – then **write the first draft without stopping to analyse** or correct what you've written and without even being sure of exactly what you're trying to say – though you may have some vague notion. Go on the journey, let all the ideas pour out, and as you do so start learning who your journey companions – your characters – are, and reach the point where you set them free to surprise you and to take twists and

turns you had never expected. Pass that point and continue on through all the unexpected deviations and contingencies and revelations – until you reach the story climax and know you have finished.

2. **Leave the draft to marinate** for a period of time; at least a number of weeks. Then come back to it, print it out, read it through, and see it afresh. **Consider the controlling idea embedded in the story climax**. It may be something very different to what you originally thought you were trying to say. Be sure you have clearly identified this idea; it must not be ambivalent. It may be negative, or positive, or ironic. But you can be sure that if you have followed your own instincts, this 'controlling idea' will be your world view. It will be true to yourself, and not to what you imagine the world around you wants to hear; not even to match what you perceive to be the beliefs of a commercial audience. The paradox is this: your story will never please anyone else if it is not true to what you really believe.

3. Then write your story in reverse. **Take your controlling idea**, write it on a Post-it Note, stick it your laptop/computer and **go through your draft again**, rewriting, setting every twist, every turning point,

every reversal, every climax of every act, in the light of that controlling idea.

Robert McKee in his book *Story* cites some examples of controlling ideas in famous films to help you understand this concept: 'Goodness triumphs when we outwit evil' (*The Witches of Eastwick*); 'The power of nature will have the final say over mankind's futile efforts' (*Elephant Man*, *The Birds*, *Scott of the Antarctic*) or 'Love fills our lives when we conquer intellectual illusions and follow our instincts' (*Hannah and her Sisters*).

In conclusion, for a story-teller, one guiding principle stands out: 'We have only one responsibility: to tell the truth.'

25 HOW CAN CARL JUNG'S THEORY OF ARCHETYPES HELP YOU IN YOUR CREATIVE WRITING?

Among his many theories, Carl Jung includes *archetypes*. An *archetype* may be defined as 'a universally understood symbol or term or pattern of behaviour'. If you read Robert McKee's *Story*, you will find that the key to writing a great novel lies in 'building archetypal elements into the story'. So what exactly are these 'archetypal elements'? And how exactly can they help creative writers?

Let me give you a few suggestions of *archetypes* from my own reading and observation:

1. **The indissoluble partnership on the quest.** This pair is hard-wired into our unconscious – Character A is the one on whom the gifts and the destiny have fallen; and Character B is the unfailingly loyal and faithful companion who provides essential moral, emotional and psychological support, without whom character A could not succeed. We see this working out in the following pairs: Frodo and Sam; Sherlock Holmes and Dr John Watson; Arthur and Merlin; The Doctor and his companion.

2. **The animal spirit guide/messenger.** We see this in the story of *Siegfried* (one of the four parts of the music drama *The Ring of the Nibelung* by Richard Wagner). As Siegfried waits for the dragon to appear he notices a woodbird in the tree, which he befriends; when he fights the dragon its blood burns his hands; licking them, he tastes the dragon blood and can understand the woodbird's song. He follows its instructions to take the Ring from the dragon's hoard. Philip Pullman extended this idea in his use of animal *daimons* in the *His Dark Materials* trilogy; Mrs Coulter has her golden monkey, and Lyra her marmoset, Pantalaimon. Here the animal is like an externalised part of our unconscious. The Bible of course makes use of this too by giving the dove a key role as a guide; and as a symbol of peace, love, the Holy Spirit. Another example is the raven. 'To have a raven's knowledge' is an Irish proverb meaning 'to have a seer's supernatural powers'. The raven was banished from the ark by Noah – but it returned later on in the Old Testament to feed Elijah in the wilderness.

3. **The saintly fool / the one who is without guile.** This character appears in the story of Parsifal again dramatised by Wagner in his opera of the same name. The fool himself, Parsifal, personifies goodness.

The quality of simplicity and purity of motive appears in many characters such as the chaplain in Joseph Heller's novel, *Catch 22*. However, Heller develops the chaplain to the point where he discovers his innocence has become irrelevant; he's disorientated by a world where killing has become a virtue. His original purity of motive, however, provides a strong emotional charge to the novel. So, too, does that of the character Dilsey, the black servant in William Faulkner's *The Sound and the Fury*. The simplicity of her approach to faith holds her together, in stark contrast to the other characters.

For a novel to be lifted from the merely 'good' to the 'great', it must incorporate archetypal elements. How can we do that? By studying great stories until this becomes part of our own subconscious as we plan and create our own.

26 HOW CAN CARL JUNG'S THEORY OF SYNCHRONICITY HELP YOU IN YOUR CREATIVE WRITING?

Among his many theories, Carl Jung includes 'synchronicity'. This may be defined as 'the meaningful patterning of two or more psycho-physical events not otherwise causally connected'. I've known of this theory for several years, and have seen it operating not only in my life but in the lives of others. Now I realise how it can help creative writers too. Let me give you a few examples of synchronicity in my own experience.

1. I saw a Ulysses Butterfly (for the first time ever) on the first day I wore a T-shirt with a Ulysses butterfly on the front (given to me by my sister several months before and not worn until that day).

2. During an Australian holiday several years later my friend wore a T-shirt whose colours and pattern exactly co-ordinated with the rainforest rock she was sitting on (confirmed later by me when I looked at the photo I took of her!)

3. A musician at the Greenbelt festival sang of childhood dreams you lose in adolescence and must hold onto, one hour after I had written out a card (in a marquee at the other end of the site in a separate event) asking God to help me fulfil my childhood dreams.

There are many other examples we can give; for example, a song came into my head and I heard it sung an hour later; I thought of a phrase, or a piece of information I needed, and a book fell off the shelf and fell open at the page containing that phrase or information; I was talking about a certain problem involving two people, and immediately the phone rang, and someone was on the other end who wanted to talk to me about that exact problem and those same two people.

Each of these contains just two psycho-physical events, but many more dramatic examples are on record, of synchronicity involving multiple events. As a footnote to my blue butterfly example above, I may say that my business card features a blue butterfly, as does my log-in icon on my computer, because both the colour blue and the freedom of the butterfly hold a symbolic significance for me.

So how can this help creative writers? Here's how – I was reading Robert McKee's book *Story* the other day; and found, among the many aspects of story structure, this phrase: 'meaning produces emotion'. 'Not money', he adds; 'not sex; not special effects; not movie stars; not lush photography'. He relates his observations to films, but they can just as easily be transposed to novels.

I recognised that behind this lies the truth that 'man abhors a vacuum'. We seek meaning above all. So much so, that the protagonist of a story can fail to achieve his object of desire, and yet we the readers and audience can still love that story. This is because (according to the skill of the story-writer) 'the flood of insight that pours from the gap delivers the hoped-for emotion but in a way we could never have foreseen'.

A synchronistic series of events often centres on 'a key image that can sum up and concentrate all meaning and emotion' – as in a great movie or novel. Consider the billboard image of Dr TJ Eckleberg, the oculist, in Scott Fitzgerald's *The Great Gatsby*; or the image of the Eye of Sauron in *The Lord of the Rings*.

Synchronistic events often incorporate images that come to us in dreams; for, of course, our dreaming minds can be the best movie directors of all. And synchronistic events can be used to great effect in a novel. But you, the story-teller, must take great care to ensure that you structure events so they don't strike the reader as random coincidence. Instead, 'let the coincidence stay and gather meaning'. Interestingly enough, this is exactly what synchronistic events do: they stay and gather meaning.

To me, all these facts of story structure serve to enhance the curious power of synchronicity. So how can I sum this up? Simply to remember, that 'meaning' supplies all the power of synchronistic events, and all the power of a great story. The art of the story-teller is only to structure his telling to serve this purpose.

27 HOW CAN CARL JUNG'S THEORY OF THE SHADOW HELP YOU IN YOUR CREATIVE WRITING?

Among his many theories, Carl Jung listed a series of archetypes. The one I want to look at in this chapter is called 'the shadow'. 'The shadow' is Jung's term for the dark side of ourselves. When we see faults in others we are typically projecting our own 'shadow' onto them. For an example of this, consider a character I created, James, who appears in both my first two novels, *Mystical Circles* and *A Passionate Spirit*, who has a 'socially acceptable' persona in which he enjoys high social status. He is now, or has been in the past, high up in the world of academia, (so far as my main protagonist can tell, by questioning him); he is an immaculate dresser, urbane, charming and turned out in Saville Row tailoring. From his neatly-combed hair, distinguished features and elegant bearing, to the details of his classic, charcoal, slim-fit suit and blue-check shirt, he looks like the sort of person who might command respect anywhere.

But is this the whole story? Imagine, if you will, that this character in fact covers deep insecurity; and that sometimes the strain of putting on a performance for the world is too great, and he then feels compelled to express the other side of his personality, 'the shadow'?

Consider a derelict, a down-and-out, a long-term homeless person, or as he may be commonly known, 'a tramp'. This person may be among the lost, the hopeless, the marginalised. Perhaps he lives in squalor. He is always dishevelled and he carries his worldly goods around with him in a well-stuffed plastic carrier bag. He never washes, and lives in filthy clothing.

This is certainly a person around whom many of those in the centre of our 'civilised' society may well feel uncomfortable, or even pretend to ignore. Here at the centre of our western consumer society there are many hunters, just as there were in the Stone Age. Only the hunters in our society hunt honour, wealth and prestige. What if any of them were to try shame and squalor instead? George Orwell did it in *Down and Out in Paris and London*. An idealistic intellectual, he took on the role of a tramp, and found out exactly what it was like to travel between 'spikes' (places where rudimentary shelter and accommodation might be offered to vagrants).

George Orwell lived out Jung's theory of 'the shadow'. As writers, we can use this powerful archetype, even without going to the lengths George Orwell did. Using the powers of empathy and imagination, we can see through the socially acceptable persona our characters may present, and we know and understand 'the shadow' that our characters try to keep hidden from those round them.

28 INSPIRATION FOR CREATIVE WRITERS FROM ARTISTS

Honesty and truthfulness – these are the outstanding virtues of a great artist. And, as a creative writer, I have in recent times found inspiration from two contemporary artists, Grayson Perry and Tracy Emin.

Both artists hold personal challenges for me; and the irony is, that in the past – perhaps in my twenties – I would have disapproved of their work (or some of it) and even found it offensive. Therefore, these two artists have a direct relevance to me, because they evoke strong reactions. Yet now their honesty compels me. And several elements of the autobiographical accounts of their social background have strong similarities to my own.

Both artists make use of phrases from our culture which they transform into art – neon signs, tapestries, lithographs, glazed vases; a vase of Grayson Perry's displays the words 'career advancement'. These words are so evocative. They carry within them all sorts of presumptions and falsehoods along with an eagerness to impress and a compulsion to present a highly-embellished picture of oneself to the world. And Tracey Emin, describing her abortion experience on film, is electrifying – simply because she is so honest.

In Grayson Perry's book *Portrait of the Artist as a Young Girl*, we find these words, an observation made by Wendy Jones who transcribed the tapes of his account: "During the interviews Grayson appeared almost physically malleable. It seemed that sometimes he would look like a First World War pilot, then a mediaeval minstrel, then a housewife suffering from ennui, then an elegant hurdler. He was always morphing – I hadn't come across that before and I doubt I shall see it often again."

This capacity to morph strikes a chord in my own experience and is described in my own novel *Mystical Circles*, where it is eventually understood as part of the shapeshifting gifts of a shaman. Wendy Jones' description was fascinating to me as I have known of those who morph in this fashion and have witnessed it myself and worked it into my own fiction.

Grayson Perry suggests that if we 'sit lightly to our beliefs', and 'let go of a compulsion to seek meaning – we will enjoy life in this world much more'. His art bears this out: everything is referred back to his childhood teddy, Alan Measles; everything set against that barometer of his childlike perceptions, even to the extent of expressing his transvestism by dressing as a little girl.

My reaction to these two artists is ironical and poignant, when I consider my own background and personal history and creative journey. Both Perry and Emin have vitally important things to say to me, and strong challenges to present. I cannot ignore these challenges as a creative writer. A writer must above all 'come clean with him or herself'.

29 INSPIRATION FOR CREATIVE WRITERS FROM MUSIC

An essential quality for great music is versatility, the power to adapt and appeal to many across boundaries of culture, class, circumstance, life event, mood and emotional state.

As a creative writer, I was reminded of this truth in an intriguing twist to my research. I was investigating 'creepy organ music' for one of the characters in my new novel. My research led me through discussions of ideal musical choices for Halloween, funerals and weddings. And I found a fascinating fact. One piece of music came up again and again in all three categories: Bach's *Toccata and Fugue in D Minor*. And this piece of music also happens to be one of my personal favourites.

Yes, Bach's music is counted as 'creepy' because it seems a popular choice for organ-playing vampires. What could be more suitable for Halloween than the faint sounds of a pipe organ being played feverishly by Count Dracula himself?

Then I pursued the idea of a 'lone organist'; words which had sprung to my mind in connection with my character, which I felt needed exploring. I learned that once again, it is Bach's *Toccata and Fugue in D Minor* that most complements the notion of an evil psychotic sitting in a hallowed place invoking the devil himself via some unholy musical ability. And this dovetails with the fact that Bach himself was a devout Christian – which again provides much cause for reflection.

Sinister, demonic, sublime, fearful, profound, uplifting, moving – one musical work which means all these things to different people. And so some deem it suitable for a wedding, while others may settle for it in the context of a funeral. Even more amusingly, however (in my eyes), although organists' guidelines in official websites lament the difficulty of persuading the family of the deceased that the favourite song of their departed loved one may not be the most suitable choice, nevertheless, the most popular funeral choice of all is 'Always Look on the Bright Side of Life', followed closely by 'My Way'.

All these discoveries provided rich inspiration for me in the development of at least two characters in my second novel, *A Passionate Spirit*. Once again, it is curious that they should strike a chord in my own background too. I find that, when you research, there are many connecting threads. Call this synchronicity, or the workings of the unconscious, or what you will; but it is one reason why research can be so enjoyable and creative in itself.

30 SUGGESTIONS FOR WRITING THE END OF A NOVEL

So important is the end, that it can spoil an otherwise excellent novel. As a regular Amazon reviewer, I have read novels thinking, "This is superb. I'm going to give this novel five stars." And then I've reached the end, and my review slips a star.

So how, as a writer, do we go about ensuring that our novel has a satisfying conclusion? For the key is in the word 'satisfying'. It's possible to write a novel having a rough idea of where you're heading and when you get there it's quite a different outcome. A novel is an organic thing. A writer may set out on the journey with the goal of exploring what it is he or she wants to say. The theme may be as yet unknown. Only by a satisfying end to the story will that theme reveal itself. Characters can change your mind. A pre-determined end turns out to be totally inappropriate. A story may have its true conclusion earlier than you had envisaged. Or too many strands are tied up neatly. You need to backtrack, finish the story at an earlier point, leaving some questions still open in the mind of a reader.

A novel may have a closed or an open ending. The end may be happy, sad, bittersweet or ironical. But certainly the end is determined by the way in which the main protagonist has pursued that over-arching desire which is the spine of the story. As Robert McKee says in *Story*, the protagonist may not achieve that desire, but 'the flood of insight that pours from the gap delivers the hoped-for emotion, in a way we could never have foreseen'.

Here are five questions to ask yourself as you consider the end of your novel:

1. Is there a **deus ex machina** in your conclusion? Or has the ending evolved from the choices made by the main protagonist? Could this ending have occurred if the protagonist had not made those choices? And does the outcome depend solely upon the inner resources of the MP, which you have developed throughout the novel, folding them through the plot in a skilful weaving of characterisation and action?

2. Have you **answered too many questions** and tied up too many loose ends?

3. Have you **said more than you needed to?** Have you failed to respect the intelligence of the reader?

4. **Is your ending a surprise?** In fact, does it top all the other surprises in the novel? Or could the reader have predicted it?

5. **Has the outcome been foreshadowed** at all? Could the reader say, "Oh yes, of

course, this makes sense because..."

Above all, we abhor a vacuum of meaning. The end of the story must have coherence, even if it's tragic, or unhappy, or ironical, or shocking. Take some great endings as an example. John Fowles' novel *The Collector* has a conclusion which penetrates the reader to the core, it is so chilling. And yet it has an organic relationship with the events of the novel and the development of the two characters. The end of *The Lord of the Rings*, JRR. Tolkien's fantasy masterpiece, is one that on many levels satisfies, and yet I personally felt it went too far. For my satisfaction, I didn't want to know about Frodo sailing away. I'd sooner it was left with the hobbits back in the Shire. But that, of course, is just my own personal response. One aspect of the ending which did greatly satisfy me was when Tolkien notes that the power of the Dark Lord is reduced and shrunk but not totally annihilated. It is still there, in a corner. It can be reawakened. I found that a profound recognition of the nature of evil in this world.

Finally, a very well-known happy ending is to be found in Jane Austen's *Pride and Prejudice*. And, yet, we are still left with the irreducible fact that Mrs Bennett and Lydia and Wickham will all continue to be problems in the future. The problems they pose will be of a slightly different nature as a result of the events of this story – but they'll still be there, because they are inextricably bound up with those characters.

31 LEARNING FROM HEMINGWAY

Ernest Hemingway said, "The most essential gift for a good writer is a built-in, shock-proof shit-detector. This is the writer's radar and all great writers have had it."

By this, Hemingway signalled the vital importance of honesty and truth in creative writing – and these two are not easily found, least of all by the writer him or herself in the very act of writing.

I have known these words of Hemingway's for two or three decades now; and on several occasions in my writing life they have come to the fore of my consciousness. Not only have I personally experienced their relevance in all the failings and triumphs of my writing life; but I see that Hemingway touches upon something so vital, it never loses its relevance and practical importance throughout a writer's life.

When I write the first draft of a novel, even if writing to a rough plan, I find that I write most fluently in the same way I used to 'waffle' in my English essays at school. That is the only way to get a first draft completed, I have discovered, in a relatively short period of time (i.e., a couple of months). The greatest challenge lies in this writer's ability to keep writing despite the fact that she strongly suspects Hemingway's shit-detector, referred to above, would probably break down through wear and tear if it ranged over any of the early drafts of her novels ....

The time for this handy device of Hemingway's to spring into action is when you come to read over your manuscript. I have found that there is nothing so exposing as creative writing. If you are a snob, or a racist, or a prude, or greedy, or morally shabby or lazy, be sure your writing will find you out. I have struggled with the things I've learned about myself which stand exposed in my own manuscript – but only when pointed out by professional editors and beta readers. This may well be one of the reasons why so many would-be writers give up. But, if you are a true writer, you'll keep going, and will get used to taking hold of 'the writer's radar' and scanning it over your manuscript. You may find that by doing this, you'll make unexpected discoveries in your tone, plot or ideas, and maybe transform your own attitude to the behaviour of your characters.

What I have learned is that in creative writing, none of us has the right to stand in judgement over the behaviour of our own characters. If we do, be sure it will register on Hemingway's detector.

Therefore, the key points of the lesson are painful and strict self-examination; followed by the guts to go forward with what you have learned, and to act on it. We all know Hemingway did that, in his writing. But I believe this applies to every writer, at whatever stage. If this were not true, the principle of what he says wouldn't keep resurfacing through the years in interviews with other great writers, reminding us of the challenge we have set ourselves.

32 ALWAYS ON THE OUTSIDE LOOKING IN: WHAT DOES A BESTSELLING NOVELIST HAVE TO TEACH ASPIRING WRITERS?

I was listening to a bestselling novelist (Howard Jacobson) speaking on the radio about his success in winning a major book award. Among the many things he said which touched and amused me, I was most impressed by the answer he gave to this question:

"Now you've won this prestigious award, do you feel you've arrived? Do you now feel you're on the inside?"

And he replied, "No. I have always felt myself to be on the outside of everything, looking in."

What a wonderful response the interviewer received to this question! And it seemed to me an authentic writer's response. As observers of human life, this is what creative writers spend their lives doing. Often whilst researching for novels, we are on the outside looking in. We do not necessarily wish to 'get involved' or 'drawn in', although there are times when we must 'come alongside' those we observe, in order to truly understand.

This is especially true of those on spiritual journeys. To be a traveller on this path, you need an open mind and an open heart, and must be prepared to go anywhere and come in on anything. This does mean exploring other spiritual outlooks, other worldviews. This should be no contradiction to a spiritual traveller, whatever religion they belong to. As Rabbi Lionel Blue discovered, 'my religion is my spiritual home not my spiritual prison'.

The great mystics have transcended religious boundaries in order to experience the presence of God beyond them all. So, how can we always be outsiders looking in? Or is it sometimes necessary to get involved, and come alongside? I believe both can co-exist simultaneously. There is, in fact, never a time when a writer is so fully involved, he or she cannot at some future time stand back and write it. Every experience, no matter how negative or difficult, can prove raw material for a writer because in the act of writing a story you are often drawing upon unconscious material. Novelist Margaret Drabble remarked that fiction writers are good at 'turning personal humiliations and losses into stories ... they recycle and sell their shames, they turn grit into pearls'.

I am particularly fascinated by group dynamics. And in order to learn about those you have to participate. But you can also observe. The truth lies in paradox. Thus the most successful creative people can literally be, in the eyes of the world, on the inside. Of course they have arrived! And yet they can still feel they are always on the outside looking in.

33 STAYING FOCUSED AS A WRITER: LEARNING FROM THE EXAMPLE OF ST PAUL

How do we stay focused when all that we hope for seems very far from being achieved? These are the words that inspire me as I write: 'Only let us live up to what we have already attained'.

They come from St Paul's letter to his Christian friends at Philippi – in the New Testament, Philippians, Chapter 3 Verse 16. It is a measure of his psychological insight that these words apply not only specifically to the individuals he wrote to, but across time and culture to any of us who aim high in any field of endeavour at all.

But, in the field of creative writing, how appropriate these words are. They are all about letting go of the negative, moving on from any feelings of inadequacy, and choosing not to focus on what hasn't worked. Earlier in this same passage, Paul says: "Forgetting what is behind and straining towards what is ahead, I press on towards the goal to win the prize." In these words, he encapsulates something which is at the heart of all success.

In the time which has passed since the publication of my first novel, several wonderful things have happened, which have either filled me with joy, or encouraged me, or which have taught me much. In addition to this, other things I hoped for have not happened – although there have been a number of intriguing flashes of hope and possibility for the future. But *only let me live up to what I have already attained*. No words could be more relevant to me at the very moment of writing this.

These words aren't passive, purely about a positive attitude, as in 'Always Look on the Bright Side of Life'. They are active, and require you to re-imagine your own story. Consider the example of Georges Méliès, French illusionist and film-maker (1861–1938). In 1923, outraged at a tragic decline in his fortunes, he personally burned all of the negatives of his films that he had stored at his Montreuil studio plus many of the sets and costumes. Later he was recognised and honoured, and received the Legion of Honour from Lumiére himself. And now two hundred of his remaining films have been released on DVD. But in that dark mood in 1923, he fell victim to a despair from which these words could have lifted him – he only needed to live up to all that he had attained.

So Paul's words remind us of our personal responsibility to acknowledge and build on all that is positive in our lives, even in the face of changeable feelings, to the extent of 'acting as if' and then finding that the feelings – of encouragement and fresh hope – follow.

ABOUT THE AUTHOR

SC Skillman was born and brought up in south London. She studied English Literature at Lancaster University. She has previously worked within a BBC production office and later spent four years in Australia. She now lives in Warwickshire with her husband David, their son Jamie and daughter Abigail.

DID YOU ENJOY THIS BOOK?

If so, why not write an Amazon review and
recommend it to other readers?

For more from SC Skillman, visit
www.scskillman.co.uk
and
www.scskillman.com

Keep up with the latest writing news at
www.facebook.com/SCSkillmanAuthor

SC Skillman on Twitter
@scskillman